My Very First Bible

Old Testament Stories
for Young Children

Retold By **L.J. SATTGAST**
Illustrated By **RUSS FLINT**

HARVEST HOUSE PUBLISHING
Eugene, Oregon 97402

MY VERY FIRST BIBLE
Old Testament Stories for Young Children

Library of Congress Cataloging-in-Publication Data

Sattgast, L. J.
    My Very First Bible: Old Testament stories for young children /
retold by L. J. Sattgast; illustrated by Russ Flint.
            p.   cm.
    Summary: An illustrated collection of forty-six Bible stories
introducing the main characters of the Old Testament.
    ISBN 0-89081-941-6
    1. Bible stories, English—O.T.   [1. Bible stories—O.T.]
I. Flint, Rull, ill.   II. Title
BS551.2.S35 1992
221.9'505—dc20   91-38563
                                                    CIP
                                                    AC

Text copyright © 1992 by L. J. Sattgast
Illustration copyright © 1992 by Russ Flint
Published by Harvest House Publishers
Eugene, Oregon 97402

Printed in the United States of America

Presented to

_____

From

_____

On

_____

Contents

In the Beginning

Genesis 1, 2

A long time ago God made the world. At first it was dark and empty.

But then God said, "Let there be light!"

The light appeared and God smiled.
"That is good," he said.

Now there was light for daytime and
dark for nighttime. This was the very
first day.

On the second
day God made
the sky above to
sit over the water
below.

On the third day God made dry land. He filled the land with plants and trees and beautiful flowers. Then he looked at it and said, "Yes, it is good!"

On the fourth day God made the sun and the moon
and the stars.
He watched the sun shine that day.
He watched the moon and the stars shine that night.
"I am pleased!" he said.

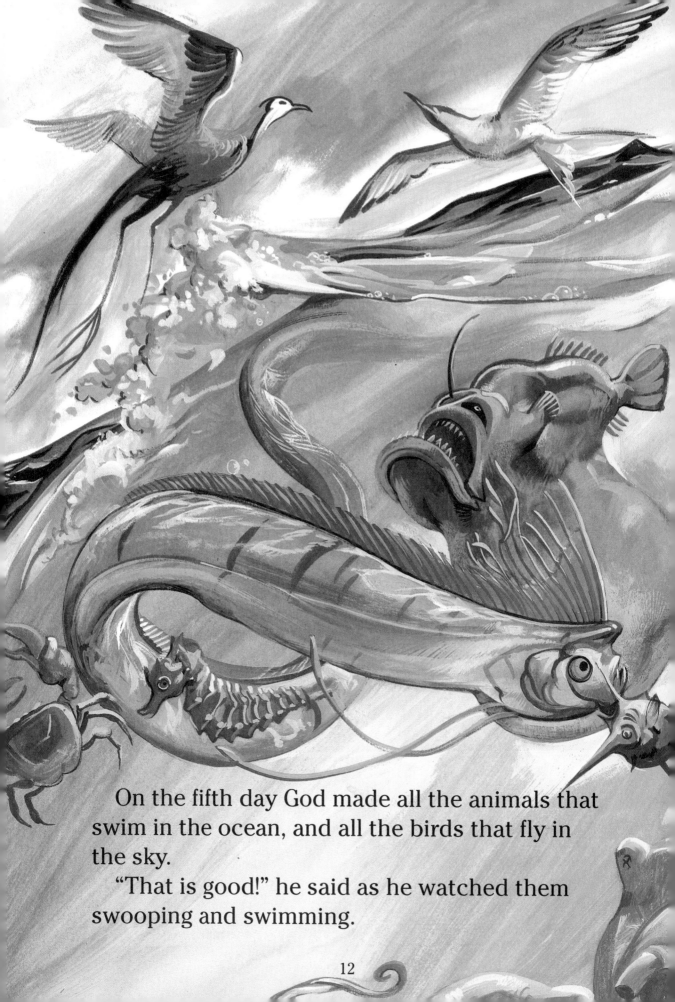

On the fifth day God made all the animals that swim in the ocean, and all the birds that fly in the sky.

"That is good!" he said as he watched them swooping and swimming.

On the sixth day God made all the animals that
walk and jump and crawl on the ground.
He liked every one of them.

But God wanted someone like himself.
"I will make people," he said, "and I will put them in charge of all the animals."
First he made a man. He called him Adam. Then he made a woman, and he called her Eve.

God saw that everything he had made was very good!

On the seventh day, God did not make anything. "One day a week is for resting," he said.

The Talking Snake

Genesis 3

God made a beautiful garden for Adam and Eve. They took care of all the plants and animals, and they ate fruit from all the trees in the garden— except one.

"Do not eat the fruit from *that* tree," said God, "because if you do, you will die!"

But the crafty snake came to Eve and said, "You will not die! If you eat that fruit, you will become as wise as God!"

Eve saw how nice the fruit looked. She reached up and picked some. Then she took a bite and gave some to Adam too.

When Adam and Eve heard God coming, they hid in the bushes.

"Where are you, Adam?" called God.
"I was afraid, so I hid," Adam answered.
"Why were you afraid?" asked God. "Did you eat the fruit I told you not to eat?"
"Eve gave me some and I ate it!" said Adam.
"Why have you done this?" God asked Eve.
"The snake tricked me, so I ate it!" said Eve.

God was sad. "You have disobeyed me and now you must leave this garden," he said.

Adam and Eve left and never went back, for God sent angels with a sword of fire to keep everyone out.

God made clothes for Adam and Eve from
the skins of animals, and from that time on
Adam and Eve had to work hard for their food.

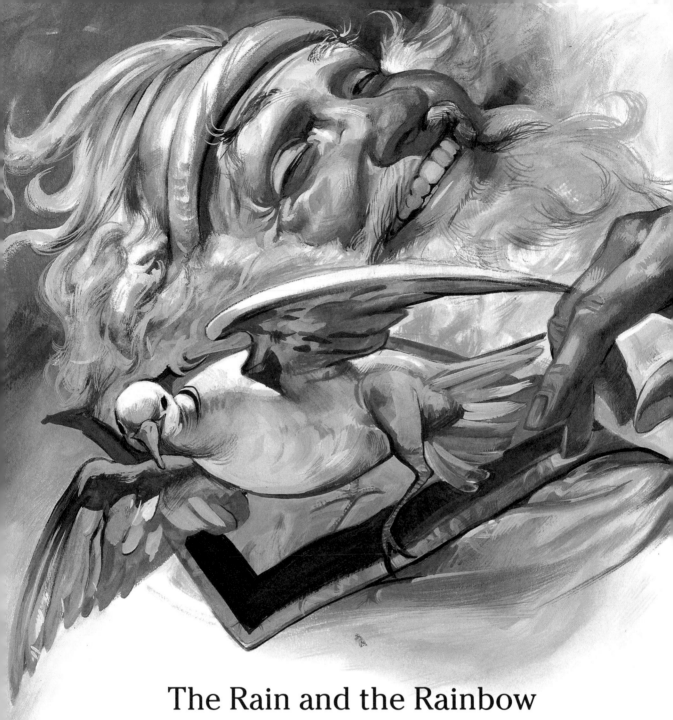

The Rain and the Rainbow

Genesis 6–9

Adam and Eve had many children. Soon the land was filled with people. But God saw all the bad things they did. "I'm sorry I ever made them!" he said.

There was only one man who still obeyed God. His name was Noah.

"Build yourself an ark," God told Noah, "because I am going to send a flood that will cover the whole earth with water."

Noah and his three sons began to build the ark right away.

When the ark was finished
the animals began to come.

The bears shuffled.
The horses neighed.
The ducks waddled.
The dogs barked.

But they all went up into the
great big ark— at least two of
every kind of animal.

When Noah and his family and all of the animals were safe inside the ark, God shut the door. Then it began to rain.

Rain poured down from the sky and water spouted up from the ground. Water splashed all around until it covered the highest mountain.

But Noah and his family and all the animals were safe and dry in the ark.

Finally the rain stopped and the water went down. The ark came to rest on a mountain, but Noah did not get out. He waited forty more days. Then he let a bird fly out the window.

When the bird came back with an olive branch in its beak, Noah knew it was almost time to leave the ark.

Noah sent the bird out again. This time it did not come back. Then Noah knew the water had gone down and it was time to get out of the ark.

Noah and his family came out of the ark. All the animals ran out into the sunshine too.

The goats skipped.

The monkeys chattered.
The donkeys brayed.
The lions stretched.
And the elephants trumpeted as if to say, "We're happy to be out too!"

Then God said to Noah, "I will never cover the whole earth with water again. Look! I have put a rainbow in the sky. Whenever you see the rainbow, it will remind you that I always keep my promises!"

Trouble Talking

Genesis 11:1–9

After the flood the land began to fill with people again. They moved away from the ark and came to a plain where the ground was flat and wide. "This looks like a good place to build a city!" they said.

The people that settled on the plain were proud. "We will build a tower that reaches up to heaven," they boasted. "Then everyone will know how important we are!"

Up, up, up went the walls as the bricklayers laid down the bricks one by one.

God saw them building the tower, and he did not like it.

"These people think they can do anything they want," he said, "but I won't let them." So he made them speak in many different languages.

"Give me some bricks," said the bricklayer.

But his helper only heard, "Babble, babble, babble."

"Why are you babbling?" asked the helper. "Can't you talk?"

But the bricklayer only heard, "Babble, babble, babble."

No one could understand anyone else, so they stopped building. They left the tower and traveled to other places.

That is why people all over the world speak different languages, and that is why the tower was called the Tower of Babel.

A Promise to Abraham

Genesis 12–15

Abraham and Sarah lived in the city of Haran.
They had lots of goats and sheep and donkeys
and camels and plenty of servants to take care
of them. But they had no children.

One day God told Abraham to leave Haran. "Start traveling," he said, "and I will show you where to go."

Abraham and Sarah and all their servants and animals started walking. When they came to the land of Canaan, God told them to stop.

One night God said, "Abraham, I will make
you into a great nation."

"But I have no children," said Abraham.

"Just look at the stars and count them if you
can," said God. "That is how big your family will
grow someday."

And Abraham believed what God said.

A Son For Sarah

Genesis 18:1–15; 21:1–7

One day Abraham had three important
visitors. "Where is your wife, Sarah?" they asked.
"She is in the tent," said Abraham.
"This time next year Sarah will have a baby,"
the visitors told Abraham.

Sarah was listening behind the tent door. "Ha!" she laughed. "I'm too old to have a baby!"

The visitors knew that Sarah had laughed, so they said, "Is anything too hard for God?"

Sure enough, a year later Sarah had a baby boy. Abraham called him Isaac.

Abraham was one hundred years old when Isaac was born.

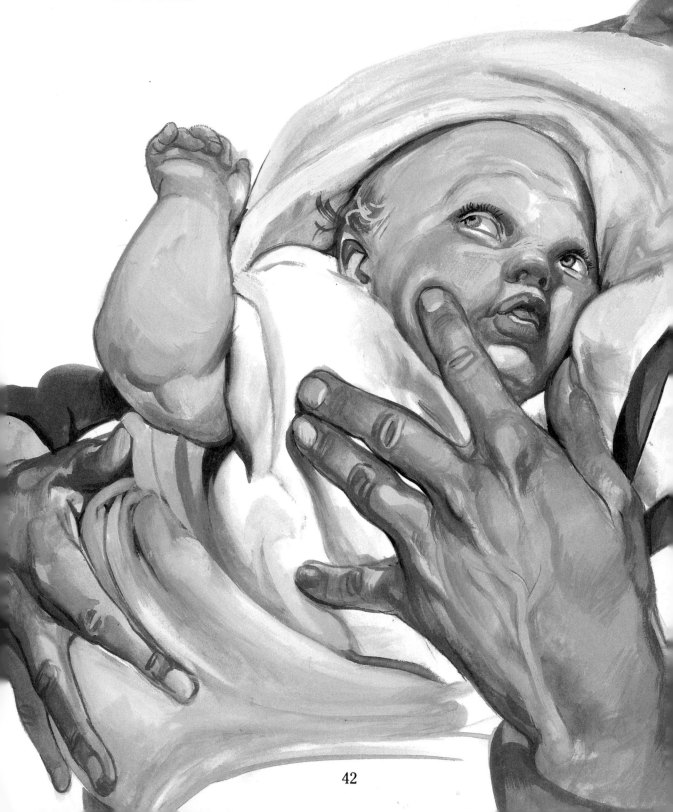

Sarah was so happy! "Who would believe that
an old woman like me would have a baby," she
said. "Now everyone who hears about this will
laugh and be happy with me!"

What the Camels Brought

Genesis 24

When Isaac grew up, Abraham called his chief servant and said, "My son Isaac is ready to get married. So go back to my relatives and find a wife for my son."

The servant packed the camels and started
on his way.

Can you count how many camels he took?

When the servant reached the town where Abraham's relatives lived, he prayed, "O Lord, help me find a good wife for Isaac."

Just then a beautiful girl named Rebekah came to the well to get water.

"Please, may I have some water to drink?" the servant asked.

Yes," said Rebekah, "and I will draw water for your camels too!"

The ten camels were happy to get a drink after their long journey!

The servant stayed with Rebekah's family. He told them why he had come. "Will you go back with me to the land of Canaan and marry Isaac?" he asked Rebekah.

What do you think she said?

She said, "Yes!"
Rebekah left her family's nice house and went to marry Isaac. They lived in a tent, and they were very happy!

Favorite Sons

Genesis 25:19–28; 27:1–40

Isaac and Rebekah had twin boys. Esau was born first. He was red and hairy, and Isaac liked him best.

Jacob was born second. His skin was smooth and fair, and Rebekah liked him best.

When the boys grew up they were as different
as the sun and the moon.

Esau hunted wild animals out in the fields, but
Jacob was a quiet man who liked to stay home.

One day Isaac said to Esau, "Go hunting and bring me back some tasty meat to eat. Then I will bless you before I die."

But when Esau left, Rebekah dressed Jacob in Esau's clothes. She put goatskin on his arms and neck to make him feel hairy.

"Now go get your brother's blessing," she said.

Isaac was old and could no longer see. But when he sniffed the clothes and touched Jacob's arms he said, "Yes, you are my son Esau!" Then he gave him this blessing:

"May God give you plenty to eat and drink, and may everyone else serve you!"

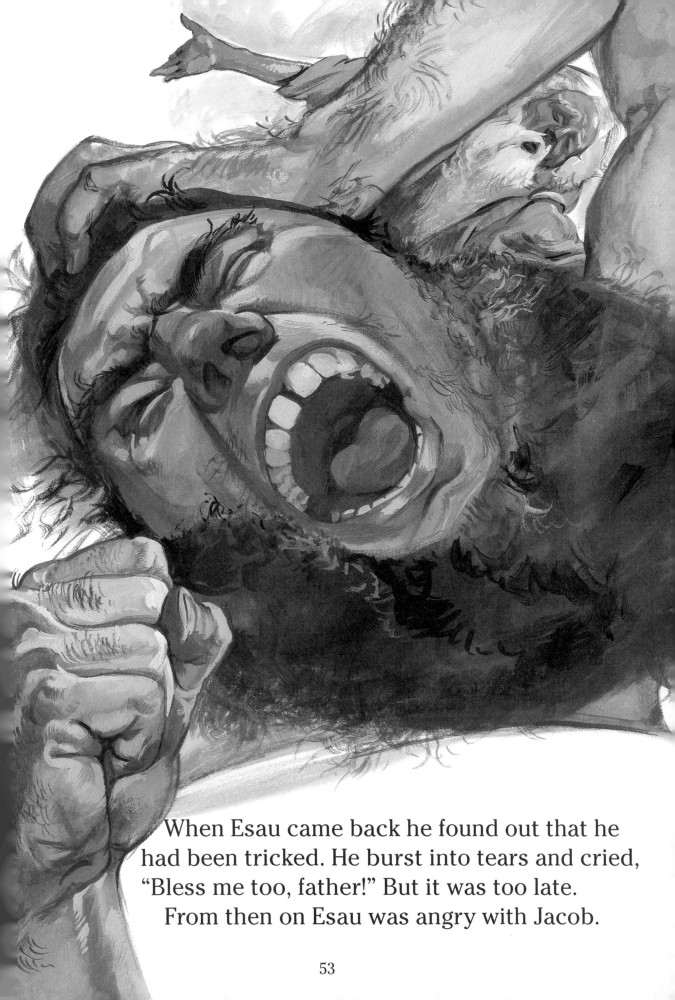

When Esau came back he found out that he had been tricked. He burst into tears and cried, "Bless me too, father!" But it was too late. From then on Esau was angry with Jacob.

Jacob's Dream

Genesis 27:42–28:22

It was time for Jacob to get married, so Isaac sent him back to Rebekah's family to find a wife.

Every day Jacob walked as far as he could. At night he slept on the ground and used a stone for a pillow.

One night Jacob dreamed he saw a ladder
that reached all the way to heaven. Angels
were going up and down the ladder, and God
was at the very top.

"I am with you wherever you go," said God,
"and I always keep my promises."

Jacob woke up. "God was here and I didn't even know it!" he said.

Jacob made a pillar out of the stone he was sleeping on. Then he poured oil on it to show that he was going to follow God.

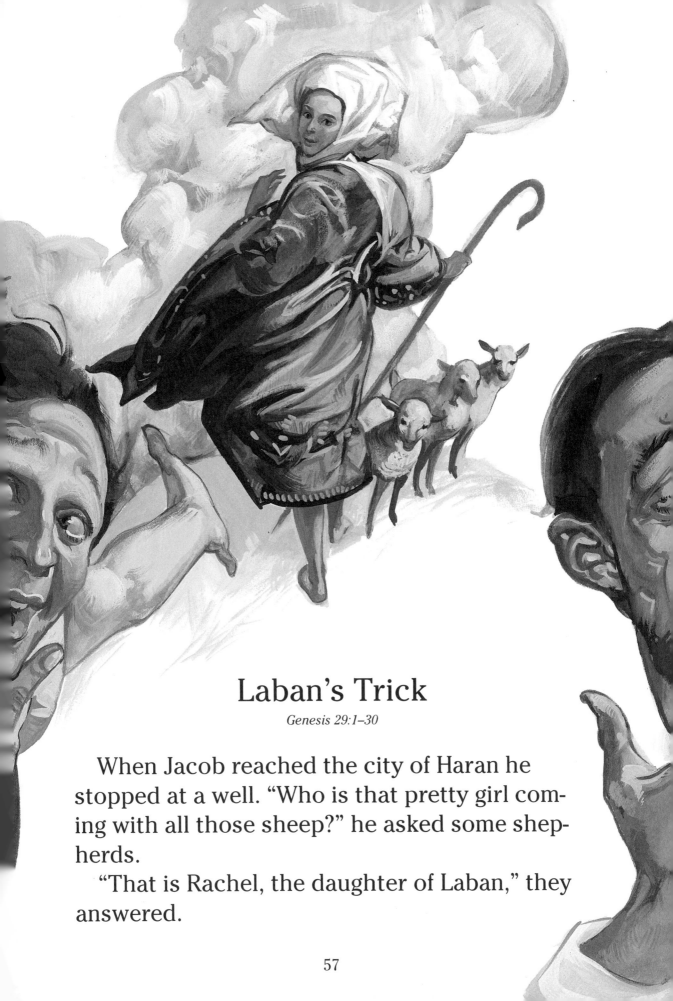

Laban's Trick

Genesis 29:1–30

When Jacob reached the city of Haran he stopped at a well. "Who is that pretty girl coming with all those sheep?" he asked some shepherds.

"That is Rachel, the daughter of Laban," they answered.

Jacob liked Rachel as soon as he saw her.
He rolled away the heavy stone that was on
top of the well and gave water to her sheep.
"Your father is my uncle," Jacob told her,
"and I have traveled a long way to see him."

Laban had two daughters. Leah was the oldest, but Rachel was the prettiest.

"I will work for you seven years if you will let me marry Rachel," said Jacob.

"All right," agreed Laban.

Seven years flew by quickly because Jacob loved Rachel so much!

Finally it was time to
get married. But after the
wedding Jacob found out
that he had married
Leah. "I've been tricked!"
he cried.

"Never mind," said Laban. "The oldest girl
should get married first, but you can marry Rachel too if you work seven more years!"

That is what Jacob did, but he always loved
Rachel more than Leah.

The Journey Home

Genesis 31–33

Look at all those sheep and goats and cows and donkeys and camels! They belong to Jacob. There he is with his shepherd's staff.
But who is he talking to?

Jacob is talking to Rachel and Leah, and this
is what he is saying:

"I have worked for your father, Laban, for
twenty years, but he isn't fair and he doesn't
like me. Now God has told me to go back to my
own country."

"You should obey God," agreed Rachel and
Leah.

Jacob took his family and everything he had and left Haran secretly without telling Laban.

When they got close to home, Jacob sent a messenger to tell Esau he was coming. Jacob was afraid that Esau was still angry at him.

But when Esau saw Jacob, do you know what he did?

He hugged and kissed Jacob and said
how glad he was to see him!

The Bad Brothers

Genesis 37

Jacob and his family settled in the land of Canaan. Jacob had twelve sons, but he loved Joseph the most. He even gave him a special coat, which made his brothers jealous.

One night Joseph dreamed that he was a star.
The sun and the moon and eleven other stars
came and bowed down to him.

Joseph's brothers were angry when they
heard the dream. "We will never bow down to
you!" they said.

One day the brothers were watching sheep when they saw Joseph coming. "Let's get rid of that dreamer!" they said.

They took his coat and threw him into a pit. "Please let me out!" cried Joseph, but his brothers would not listen.

When a caravan of camels
came by, the bad brothers sold
Joseph to one of the men.

The men took him far away
from his home.

Poor Joseph! Aren't you glad
that God was still with him?

Joseph in Prison

Genesis 39, 40

Joseph was a slave in Egypt. He belonged to a rich man named Potiphar. See how hard he is working! He must do whatever Potiphar tells him to do.

Joseph worked so hard that Potiphar put him in charge of his whole house. "I know that God is with you," said Potiphar.

But one day Potiphar's wife lied about Joseph. "This slave tried to hurt me!" she cried.
Potiphar was angry and sent Joseph to prison.

Even in prison Joseph was a hard worker. Soon he was put in charge of all the other prisoners.

One morning Joseph noticed that two of the other prisoners were sad.

"What's the matter?" he asked.

"We each had a dream," they replied, "and we don't know what the dreams mean."

"God can tell you what dreams mean!" Joseph said. Then he explained their dreams. "One of you will go free tomorrow, but the other will die."

The next day the dreams came true. "Help me get out of prison," said Joseph to the man who was set free. But the man forgot about Joseph.

Pharaoh's Dream

Genesis 41

King Pharaoh called all the wise men of Egypt together. "I had a dream last night," he said. "Now tell me what it means."

They all nodded their heads and looked wise.

"In my dream I saw seven fat cows coming up out of the Nile River," said Pharaoh.

"Then seven ugly, thin cows came and ate up the fat cows, but the thin cows did not get any fatter. Now tell me what this means."

The wise men thought and thought, but they could not explain the dream to Pharaoh.

One of the king's servants said, "I know
a man who can explain dreams."

"Send for him at once!" ordered Pharaoh.

Soon Joseph was standing before Pharaoh.
"God will help me explain your dream," he said.

"The seven good cows mean that Egypt will have seven good years with plenty of food."

"The seven bad cows mean that seven bad years will come next, when there will not be enough food for all the hungry people to eat."

"You must find a wise man to collect food during the good years," said Joseph. "Then when the bad years come, there will be enough to eat."

"Who is wiser than you?" said Pharaoh. "I will put you in charge of collecting the food!"

Pharaoh gave his ring to Joseph and dressed him in fine clothes. He gave him a chariot to ride in, and everyone had to do what Joseph said.

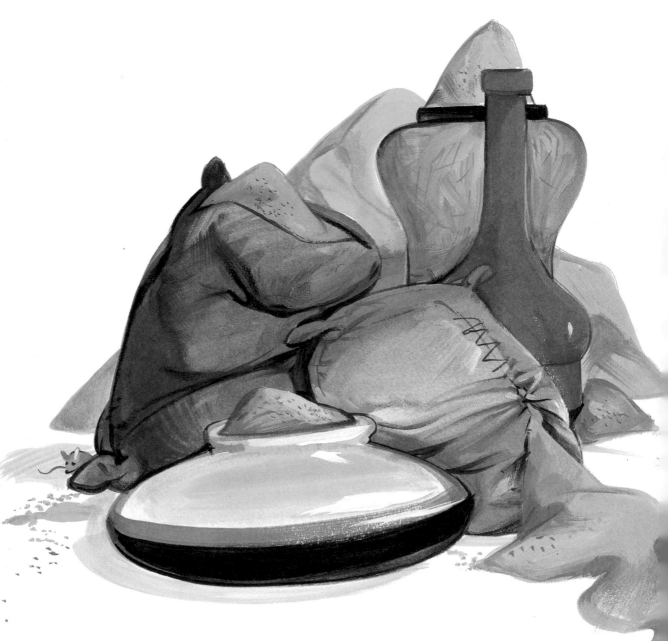

The Brothers Bow Down

Genesis 41:46–46:30

Joseph collected food during the seven good years. There were so many sacks of grain that he could no longer count them.

Then the seven bad years began. The rain did not fall and food would not grow.

Many people came to Joseph for food.

One day Joseph was surprised to see his ten brothers coming to buy food. Did they know who he was? No! They bowed down to him.

Joseph pretended to be angry. "You are spies!" he said.

"We are not spies!" said the brothers. "We live
in Canaan with our father and younger brother.
We only came to buy food!"

"All right," said Joseph. "I will give you food
this time. But if you come again, you must bring
your younger brother so I know that you are
telling the truth."

When it was time to buy
more food, Benjamin, the
youngest brother, went too.
Jacob was sad.
"Don't let anything happen
to Benjamin!" he cried.

When Joseph saw Benjamin he invited the
brothers to eat with him, but he still did not tell
them who he was.

After they ate he sent them away with sacks
of food. But Joseph told his servant to hide his
silver cup in Benjamin's sack.

The brothers had not gone far when Joseph's servants caught up with them. "Who stole our master's cup?" they demanded.

They looked in every sack and finally found it in Benjamin's sack.

Joseph acted angry when they came back. "Benjamin will be my slave!" he said.

"Oh, please, sir!" the brothers begged. "Our father will die if you keep Benjamin!"

Then they whispered to each other, "God is punishing us for what we did to Joseph."

Joseph could not pretend any longer. He sent the servants away. Then he burst into tears.

"I am Joseph, your brother!" he cried.

At first the brothers were afraid, but Joseph said, "Don't be afraid! You did something bad, but God turned it into something good. Now I can give you all the food you need."

So Jacob and all his family went to live in Egypt. When Jacob saw Joseph he hugged and kissed him. "I never thought I would see you again!" he said.

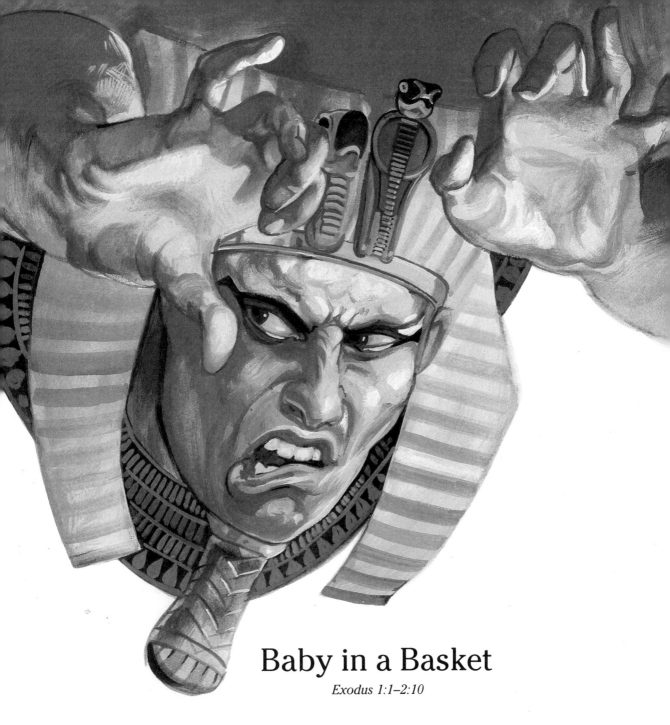

Baby in a Basket

Exodus 1:1–2:10

Jacob's sons were called the children of Israel.

After many years a new Pharaoh became king. "There are too many Israelites!" said the new king. So he made a rule:

Every baby boy that is born to an Israelite family must be thrown into the river.

What a wicked king he was!

This mother had a baby boy. She loved her little boy and did not want to throw him into the river. What should she do?

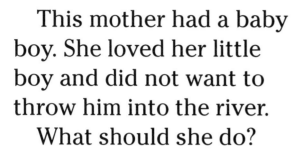

At first she tried to hide him. But that did not work very well.

So the mother got a basket. She covered it with tar and pitch.

Then she put her little boy in the basket and let it float on the river.

The little boy's sister hid in the reeds nearby to see what would happen to her baby brother.

Just then Pharaoh's daughter came down to the river to take a bath.

"Go get that basket," she said to her servant. "I want to see what is in it."

When she looked in the basket she saw a baby boy. "Waah! Waah!" he cried.

Pharaoh's daughter felt sorry for the baby!

The baby's sister came out of her hiding place.
"Should I go get someone to nurse him for you?"
she asked.

"Yes!" replied Pharaoh's daughter.

Guess who the sister ran to get?

She went to get their very own mother! His
mother took care of him, and when he was old
enough he went to live in King Pharaoh's palace.
Pharaoh's daughter called the boy Moses.

The Bush that Didn't Burn

Exodus 2:11–4:23

When Moses grew up he saw how cruel the Egyptians were to the children of Israel.

Moses tried to help his people, but Pharaoh became angry with him. So Moses ran away into the desert.

Moses lived with a shepherd in the desert. Year after year he took care of the sheep. He grew old and his hair turned gray.

Every day was about the same as any other. Then one day something strange happened.

Moses saw a bush burning with fire, but it did not burn up. Then he saw that God was in the fire!

God said, "Moses, Moses!"

And Moses said, "Here I am."

Then God said, "I want you to bring the children of Israel out of Egypt."

But Moses was afraid. "What if they won't listen to me?" he said.

"What do you have in your hand?" asked God.

"A staff," replied Moses.

"Throw down your staff," God commanded.

When Moses threw down his staff it turned into a snake! Moses was afraid and ran away.

"Now pick up the snake," said God. What do you think happened?

The snake turned back into a staff again!
"If the children of Israel don't believe you,"
said God, "show them this miracle!"
So Moses got ready to go back to Egypt.

Ten Terrible Plagues

Exodus 5–12

Moses went to Pharaoh in Egypt.
"God says to let his people go!" said
Moses.

But Pharaoh just laughed. "I don't know
God," he said, "and I will not let them go!"

After that Pharaoh made the Israelites work even harder.

"You are lazy!" he said. "From now on you must find your own straw to make bricks."

The Israelites came to Moses and said, "Now Pharaoh hates us even more!"

So Moses prayed and God answered, "I will send ten terrible plagues to Egypt, and after that Pharaoh will let my people go!"

The first plague God sent was on the rivers. The water turned to blood and no one could drink it.

Then God sent a plague of frogs. There were frogs everywhere! But did Pharaoh listen to God? No, he did not!

Then God sent a plague of gnats to bite and sting the people and the animals.

But Pharaoh still did not listen, so God sent a plague of flies.

Buzzzzzzz–swat! How the Egyptians hated those flies!

Pharaoh still would not let the people go, so God sent a plague on the animals. The horses and donkeys and camels and sheep and goats began to die.

Do you think Pharaoh decided to obey God? No, he did not!

So God sent a plague of sores. Pharaoh had so many sores that he could hardly sit up. But he still would not listen to Moses.

So God sent a plague of hail. Lightning flashed and ice came down from the sky. Pharaoh did not like it at all.

Then God sent a plague of locusts. They ate the grass and leaves and left every branch bare.

Pharaoh still would not listen, so God made the sky dark in the middle of the day!

Pharaoh was angry. "Don't ever come see me again!" he told Moses.

"All right," said Moses. "I won't come again."

"I will send one more terrible plague," said God. "So listen carefully and do what I say!

"Each family must put some blood from a lamb on the top and side of the door. Then they must eat a special dinner called the Passover meal."

So the Israelites did as God told them.

That night God went through the land of Egypt. He passed right over every house with blood on the door. But the oldest son in each house of the Egyptians died.

The Egyptians wailed and cried.

Pharaoh sent for Moses. "Go away!" he said, "and take all the Israelites with you!"

The Great Chase

Exodus 12:31–15:21

The children of Israel left Egypt in a hurry.
During the day God led them by a pillar of cloud.
And at night God led them by a great pillar of fire
so that they could see where to go.

Then Pharaoh changed his mind. "Why did I let the Israelites go?" he said. "Now who will do all the work?"

So Pharaoh's soldiers chased after them.

The Israelites were camped by the sea.
When they saw the army of Egypt chasing
them, they were afraid.
But God said, "Don't worry."

That night God told Moses to stretch his hand out over the sea. Moses held out his hand, and a strong wind began to blow.

All night the wind blew the sea back.
By early morning there was a dry path
right through the sea! The Israelites
walked safely across to the other side.

"Follow the Israelites!" shouted the Egyptians.
But Moses held out his hand again. Down
crashed the water on top of the Egyptians!
Then all the women danced for joy and sang,

"God has saved us from the Egyptians.
No one is as great and strong as our God!"

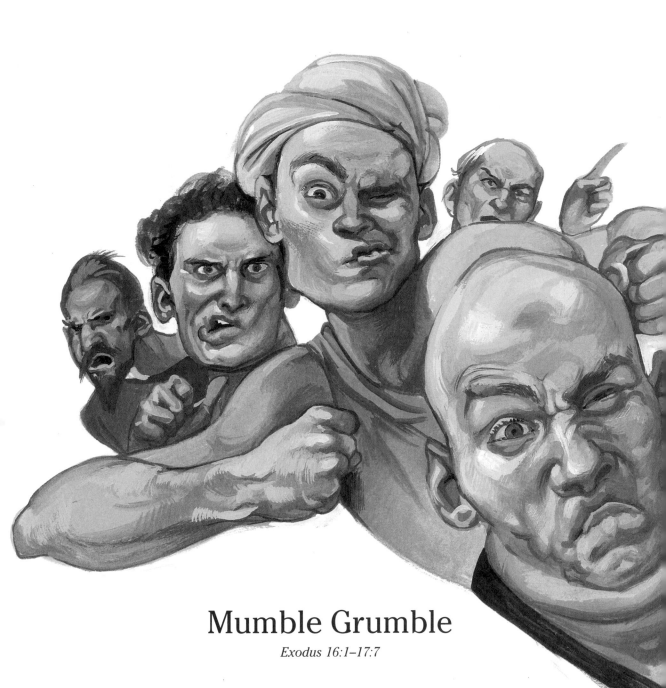

Mumble Grumble

Exodus 16:1–17:7

Moses led the children of Israel into the Sinai desert. It was hot. It was dusty. And the people were hungry.

"We don't have enough food," complained the people. "We will all die!"

"God has heard your grumbling," said Moses, "and he will send you food."

That evening a flock of quail landed in the camp. The people caught them and had quail for supper.

And in the morning the ground was covered with something white. Was it snow? No, it was bread! The people called it manna.

"Now we are thirsty!" grumbled the people.

"What shall I do?" cried Moses.

"Hit that big rock with your staff," said God. When Moses hit the rock, water came gushing out. The people jostled and splashed and dipped and drank until everyone had enough.

But God was not pleased with the way they grumbled and complained.

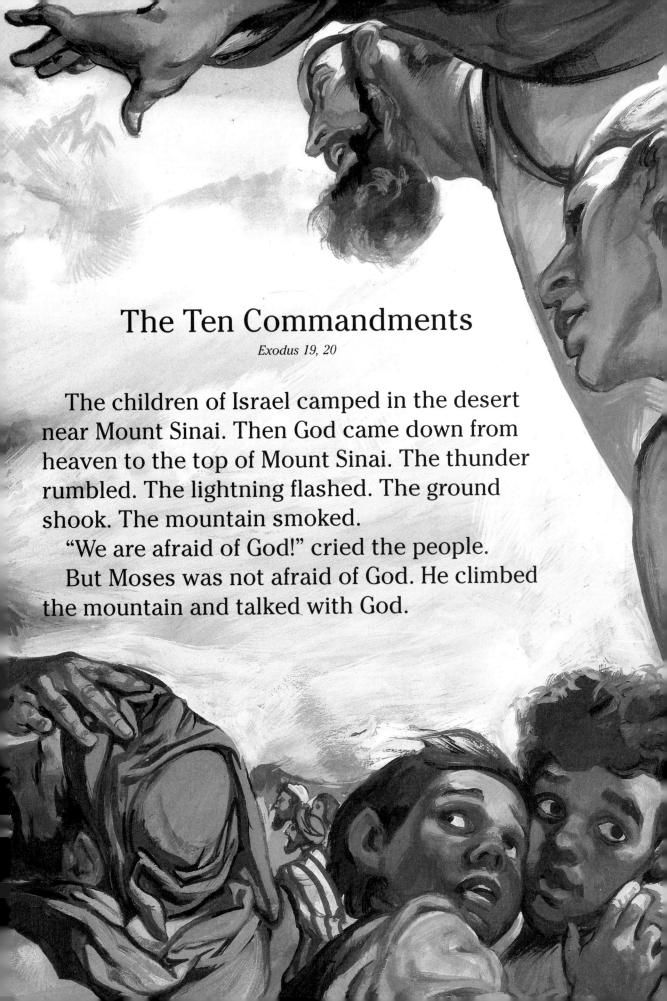

The Ten Commandments

Exodus 19, 20

The children of Israel camped in the desert near Mount Sinai. Then God came down from heaven to the top of Mount Sinai. The thunder rumbled. The lightning flashed. The ground shook. The mountain smoked.

"We are afraid of God!" cried the people.

But Moses was not afraid of God. He climbed the mountain and talked with God.

This is what God said:

Don't worship
anyone but God.

Never bow down
to idols.

Never say God's
name in a bad way.

Remember to rest
on the Lord's day.

Obey your father
and your mother.

Don't ever get angry
and kill someone.

Enjoy your own wife
or husband, and don't
go after someone else's.

Don't steal things
from other people.

Don't tell lies
about other people.

Don't wish
for someone
else's things.

God wrote the Ten Commandments on two
tablets of stone for Moses.

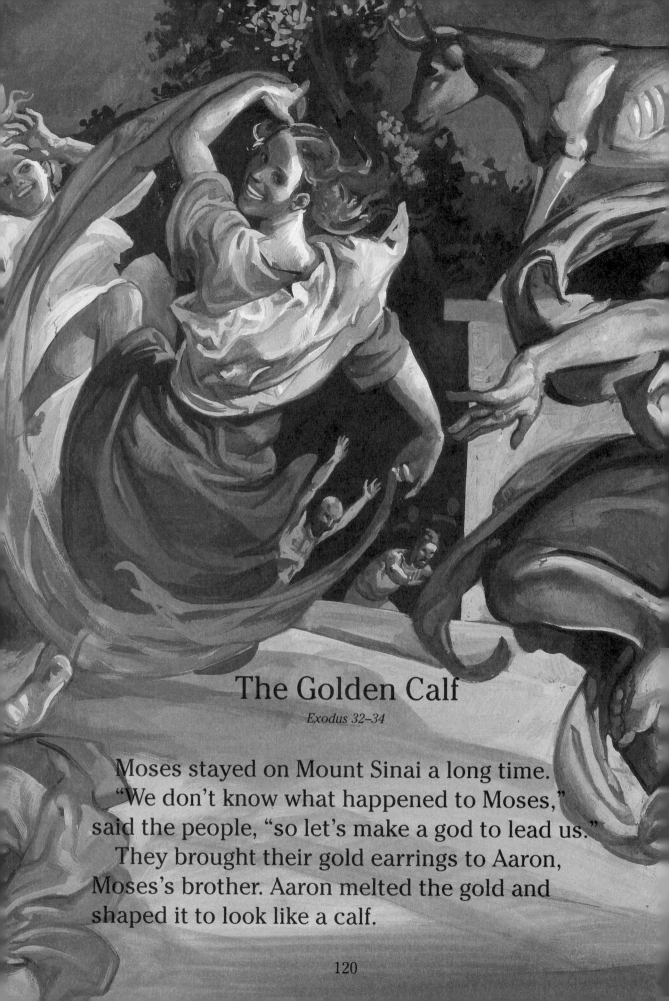

The Golden Calf

Exodus 32–34

Moses stayed on Mount Sinai a long time. "We don't know what happened to Moses," said the people, "so let's make a god to lead us." They brought their gold earrings to Aaron, Moses's brother. Aaron melted the gold and shaped it to look like a calf.

The people bowed down to the golden calf.
They pretended that the calf had brought them
safely out of Egypt. They danced and sang and
had a wild party.

"Go back down the mountain," God told Moses.
"The people are doing something bad."

Moses went back down to the camp. When he saw the golden calf he was angry. He threw down the tablets with the Ten Commandments written on them, and they broke into pieces at the foot of the mountain.

"What have you done?" cried Moses to his brother Aaron.

"Don't be angry with me," said Aaron. "The people made me do this."

Moses ground the golden calf into fine powder. He put the powder in water and made the people drink it.

Moses went back up to Mount Sinai. "The people have done a very wicked thing," he said to God. "Please forgive them. Do not be angry and do not leave us."

"I will stay with you," said God. Then once again he wrote the Ten Commandments on two stone tablets for Moses.

The Tabernacle

Exodus 35–40

Moses called all the Israelites together. "We are going to build a tabernacle where we can worship God," he said.

So the people brought offerings to help with the building. They brought so much that Moses finally said, "Stop! We have too much!"

Then the workers went to work. They wove cloth.

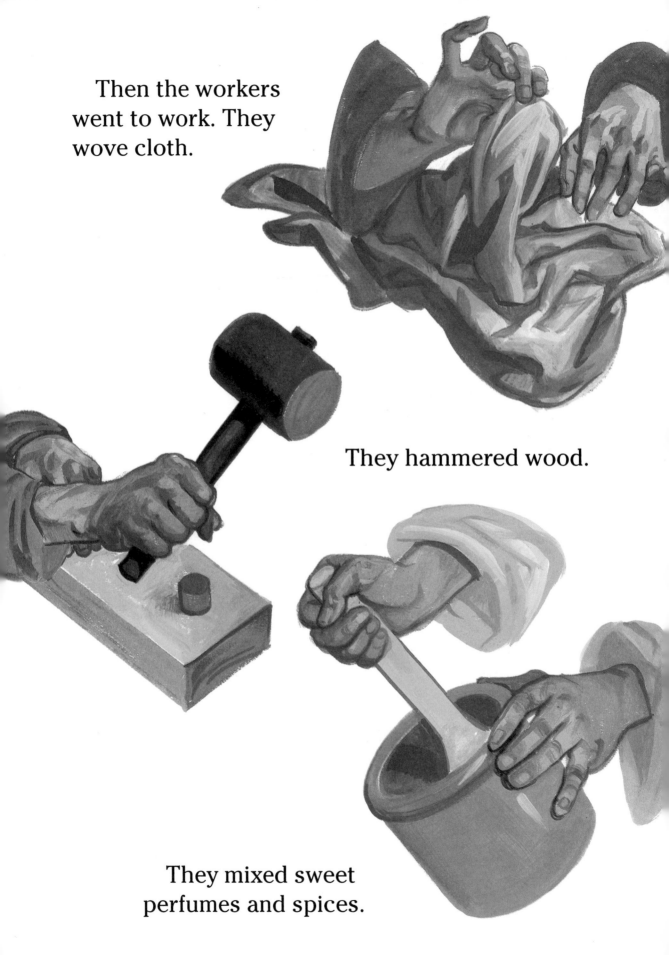

They hammered wood.

They mixed sweet perfumes and spices.

They melted and shaped the gold.

They sewed clothes for the priests.

They all worked together until the tabernacle was done.

Then the glory of the Lord came down like a cloud and filled the tabernacle.

As long as the cloud was there, the people stayed where they were. But when the cloud lifted, they knew it was time to move on.

Giants and Grasshoppers

Numbers 13, 14

The children of Israel were close to the land God had promised to give them. What would their new home be like?

Moses picked out twelve men. "Go explore the land of Canaan," he said. "Then come back and tell us what you saw."

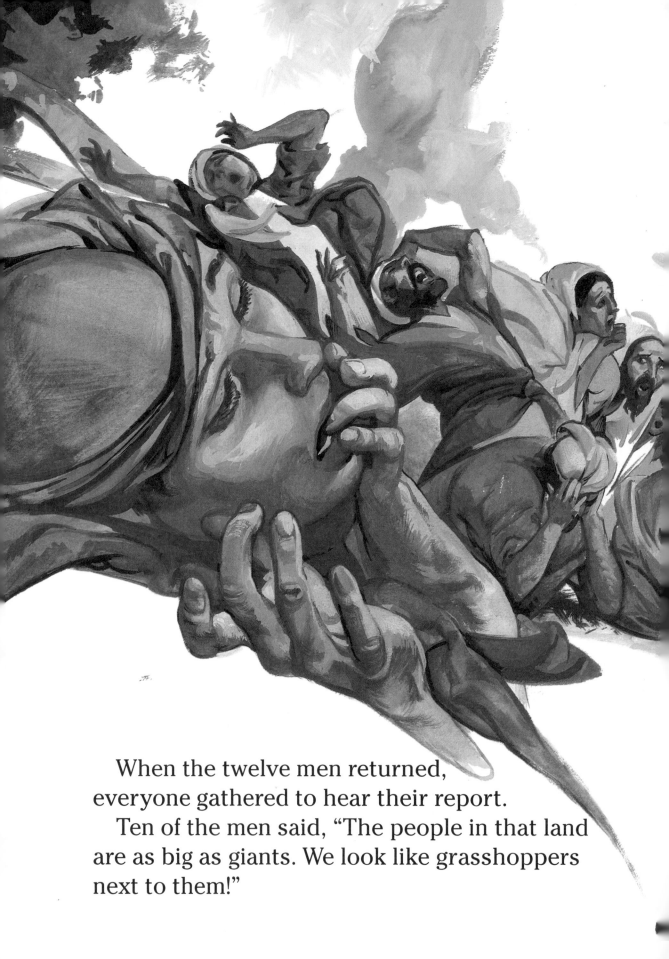

When the twelve men returned,
everyone gathered to hear their report.
    Ten of the men said, "The people in that land
are as big as giants. We look like grasshoppers
next to them!"

But Joshua and Caleb said, "The land is good. Just look at this big bunch of grapes we picked! We should not be afraid because God is with us."

Then the children of Israel grumbled and said, "Let's go back to Egypt!"

God was angry with them for grumbling.
"Since you don't believe me," he said, "I will
not let you go into the land of Canaan. You will
wander around in the desert for forty long years.
Then when your children are grown, I will take
them into the land."
And that is exactly what happened.

A New Leader

Joshua 1, 2

When Moses died, Joshua became the new
leader. Right away he sent two spies to look at the
land of Canaan. "Tell me what you find," he said.

The spies went to Jericho where they met a woman named Rahab. "May we stay in your house?" they asked.

And Rahab let them stay.

Soon the king's soldiers banged on Rahab's door. "Where are the two men who came to your house?" the soldiers hollered. "They are spies who want to take over our city!"

"They already left," she answered, "but you can catch them if you hurry!"

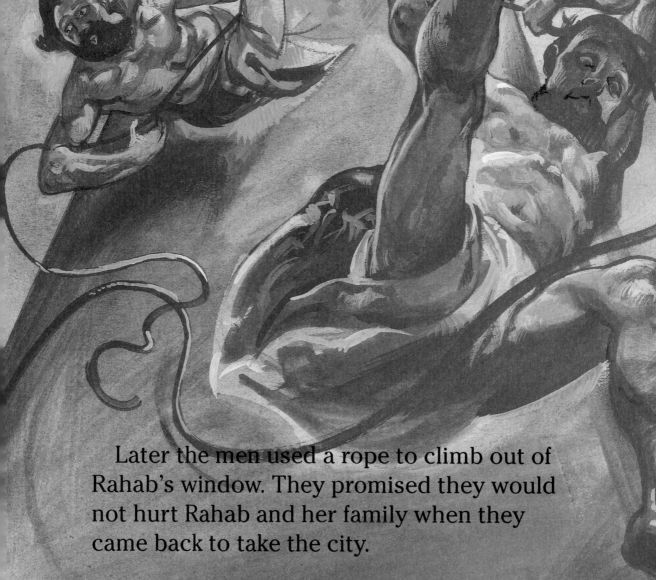

Do you know where the
two spies really were?
Rahab had hidden them
under some straw!

Later the men used a rope to climb out of
Rahab's window. They promised they would
not hurt Rahab and her family when they
came back to take the city.

The Walls Fall Down

Joshua 3–6

It was time for the Israelites to go into the land of Canaan.

"God has given us this land," said Joshua, "because the people there are wicked. We must fight for it, but God will help us."

The first city they went to was Jericho. The wall around Jericho was tall and strong.

Should they try to climb over it? Should they knock it down?

No. God told them to march around the city.

Six days in a row the people marched around Jericho. On the seventh day they marched around Jericho seven times.

Then the priests blew their trumpets and all the people SHOUTED!

What do you think happened?

God made the walls go tumbling
down! Now the city was theirs, but
they remembered to be kind to
Rahab and her family.

Too Many Men

Judges 6, 7

This man's name is Gideon. He is hiding while he works. Do you know why?

It is because he is afraid of the Midianites.

One day Gideon saw an angel. "God is with you, mighty soldier," said the angel.

Gideon was surprised. "If God is with us, then why does he let the people of Midian steal our crops and food?" he asked.

"God wants you to drive the Midianites away!" replied the angel.

Gideon gathered a great army of men.
  "Your army is too big," God told him. "Tell the
men to drink some water from the river."

Most of the men kneeled down and drank water from the river.

But some of the men lapped water out of their hands like a dog.

"I choose only the few men who lapped like a dog," said God. "Then you will know that I was the one who won the battle!"

That night Gideon and his men came creeping quietly up to the Midianite camp. Then suddenly they lifted their torches and blew their trumpets. The Midianites were so afraid that they ran away and stopped bothering the Israelites!

The Strongest Man

Judges 13–16

Samson was the strongest man in Israel.
"Don't ever cut your hair," God told him, "or
you will lose your strength."

One day Samson saw a pretty woman. Her name was Delilah.

"I like her!" said Samson. He did not care that she was a Philistine, an enemy of Israel.

The Philistine leaders came to Delilah.
"We will give you many silver coins if you can find out why Samson is so strong," they said.

Day after day Delilah asked Samson why he was so strong. Samson grew tired of her questions. "All right!" he said. "I will tell you my secret. The day I cut my hair I will become as weak as any other man!"

That night, while
Samson was sleeping,
the Philistines cut off
his hair.

Samson woke up and tried to fight, but he was
no longer strong.

The Philistines gouged out his eyes and made
him work hard grinding grain.

One day the Philistines had a great feast. "Bring Samson out so we can laugh at him!" shouted the people. They did not realize that Samson's hair had grown long again.

Samson prayed, "Help me, God." Then he
pushed on two pillars with all his might.
Down came the building with a mighty crash!
Samson and all the Philistines died.

Ruth Finds a Home

Book of Ruth

Naomi had left the land of Israel, but now she was going back. "Good-bye," she said as she hugged her two daughters-in-law.

Orpah kissed her and left. But Ruth would not leave. "I will go wherever you go," she said.

Ruth and Naomi went back to Israel.

"Look who's back!" cried the people. "Can it be Naomi?"

"I left with my family," said Naomi, "but now my husband and two sons are dead. Ruth, my daughter-in-law, is all I have left."

Now it happened to be the time for harvest. "I want to help get food," said Ruth. So she walked in the fields and gathered grain left over by the workers.

Boaz was the owner of the field. "Who is that young woman gathering grain?" he asked.

"That is Ruth," they replied. "She is the daughter-in-law of Naomi."

"Make sure you leave plenty of grain for her," said Boaz.

Naomi was pleased with all the grain.
"Boaz is a relative of mine," she said.
Then she told Ruth what to do.

Ruth did as Naomi said. She secretly
went to Boaz. "Will you marry me?"
she asked.

Boaz was surprised and glad. "You
could have gone after a much younger
man," he said.

So Ruth and Boaz were married, and
after awhile they had a little boy.
Naomi was such a proud grandmother.
"God has made me very happy!" she said.

A Boy Listens

1 Samuel 1–3

Hannah lived in a good home and she had a fine husband. But she cried because she had no children.

"Don't be sad, Hannah," said her husband.

But Hannah cried anyway.

Every year Hannah and her husband went to the tabernacle to worship God.

One year Hannah prayed, "Dear God, if you will give me a son, I will give him back to you!"

God answered Hannah's prayer and gave her a baby boy. She named him Samuel.

When Samuel was old enough,
Hannah took him to the tabernacle.
   "I am giving my son back to God, just
like I promised!" she said to Eli the Priest.
So Samuel stayed and helped Eli.

One night Samuel heard someone call his name.
He ran to Eli and said, "Here I am!"

"I did not call you," said Eli. "Go back to bed."

Then Samuel heard his name again. He ran to
Eli, but Eli had not called.

When it happened again, Eli knew who was
calling. He told Samuel what to do.

Samuel heard his name again, "Samuel!
Samuel!" said the voice.

"Speak, Lord," said Samuel. "I'm listening!"

Then God told Samuel many things that would
happen someday.

Samuel grew up to be a great prophet.
When God wanted to tell the people of Israel
something, he told Samuel, and Samuel told
the people.

Aren't you glad Samuel listened to God?

The Tall King

1 Samuel 8–10

When Samuel grew old the people came to him and said, "We want a king like all the other nations around us."

Samuel was not pleased, but God said, "Go ahead and give them a king."

At that time there was a man named Saul who was a head taller than everyone else.

One day Saul's father said, "My donkeys are lost. Please go look for them."

Saul hunted three days for the donkeys, but he could not find them anywhere.

Finally Saul went to see Samuel. "Perhaps he can tell me where they are," he thought.

"Do not worry about the donkeys," said Samuel. "They have been found."

Then Samuel poured oil on Saul's head. "God wants you to be the first king of Israel," he said.

All the people gathered together to see the new king.

But Saul was afraid and hid among the baggage!

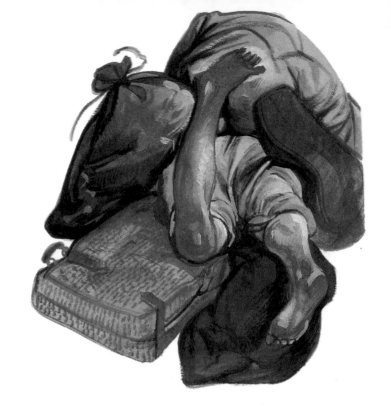

The people ran and brought him out. "Long live the king!" they shouted.

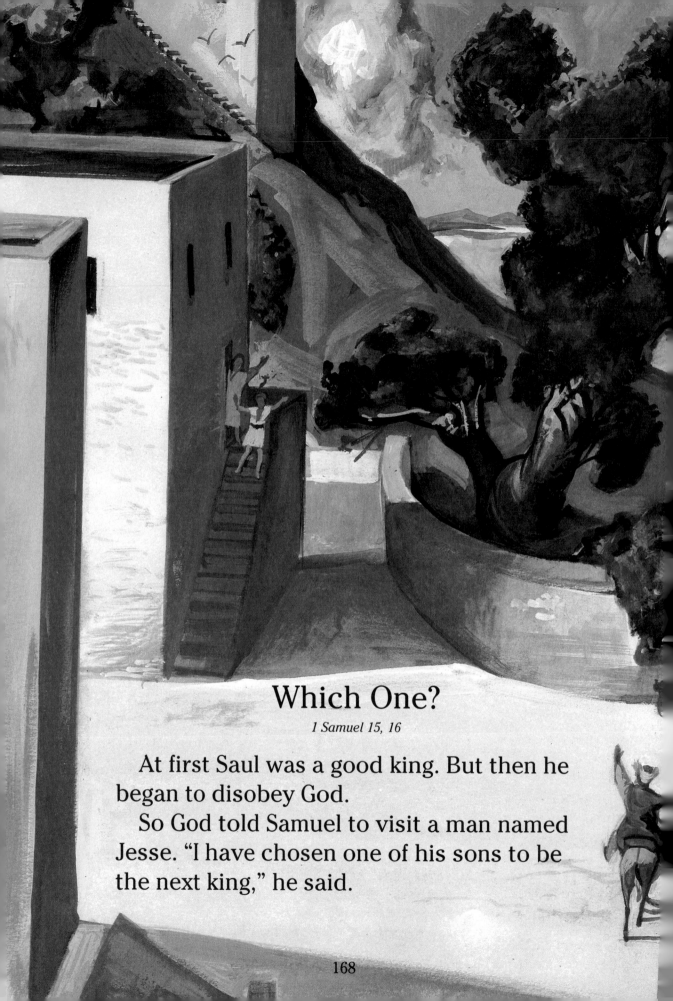

Which One?

1 Samuel 15, 16

At first Saul was a good king. But then he began to disobey God.

So God told Samuel to visit a man named Jesse. "I have chosen one of his sons to be the next king," he said.

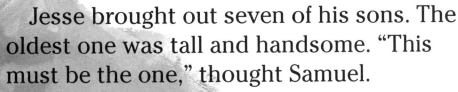

Jesse brought out seven of his sons. The oldest one was tall and handsome. "This must be the one," thought Samuel.

But God did not choose him.

One by one Samuel looked at Jesse's sons, but God did not choose any of them.

"Do you have any more sons?" asked Samuel. "My youngest son is out taking care of the sheep," replied Jesse. "His name is David." "Send for him right away," said Samuel.

When David came, God said, "This is the one!"
So Samuel poured oil on David's head.

From that time on, God's Spirit came to stay
with David.

The Shepherd

1 Samuel 17:34, 35; Psalm 23

David was a shepherd. He had
a staff and a sling, and he carried his
lunch in a pouch.

All day long David took care of the
sheep. He showed them where they
could find tender shoots of grass to eat.
He watched the little lambs skip and play
near their mothers.

When the sheep were thirsty, David would lead them to a quiet stream of water. How cool the water felt on a hot sunny day!

Sometimes David used his sling to scare away hungry lions and bears. The sheep felt safe when David was near!

At night the sheep would settle down to sleep. They snuggled together to keep warm. Then David would look up at the stars and play a lullaby for them on his harp. He sang songs about God, who took care of him like a shepherd takes care of his sheep.

God Is Great

Psalm 104

David sang many wonderful songs about God.
Here is one of them:

O God, you are very great!
You dress in a robe of light,
and you stretch out the sky like a tent.
You ride on the clouds,
and the wind whispers your words.

You made the earth and dressed it
with mountains and seas.
Springs of water pour into the valleys.
The wild animals have plenty to drink.
Birds nest in the trees and sing sweetly
among the branches.

God makes the plants grow—
green grass for cows to munch
and plants for food and bread,
so that everyone
can have enough to eat.

All day long
While I work and play
I will think about God.
I will sing songs of praise,
for God is very great!

A Boy and a Giant

1 Samuel 17

Goliath was big. Goliath was strong. "Come and fight me if you dare!" he shouted to the Israelites.

But the Israelites were afraid to fight Goliath. They all ran away.

One day David, the son of Jesse, came
to the Israelite camp. He was bringing
food for his brothers.

David heard what Goliath said and saw
that the soldiers were afraid.

Then David heard something else.

"The king will give a lot of money to the man who kills Goliath," said some soldiers. "He will let him marry his daughter. And he will never have to pay taxes."

"Why should this man shout against God's people?" said David. "I will fight Goliath!"

David's brothers were angry. "Go back and take care of your few sheep!" they said.

But David paid no attention to them.

When Saul heard about David he tried to give him his armor, but it didn't fit.

"I'm not used to these," said David, and he took them off.

David picked up five smooth stones from
the stream. He put them in his shepherd's pouch.
Then David ran toward Goliath.

Goliath was angry. "So, they sent a boy to fight me!"
he roared. "Come here and I'll feed you to the birds!"

David said, "You trust in your sword and spear, but
I trust in God!"

David took a stone from his pouch. He put it
in his sling and swung it around and around.
Then he threw the stone at Goliath.

Thunk! The stone hit Goliath right on the
forehead. Down crashed Goliath to the ground!

Two Friends

1 Samuel 18–20

Jonathan was the son of King Saul. He and David became good friends.

But Saul did not like David. He knew that God had chosen David to be king.

Whenever Saul didn't feel well, he asked David
to play his harp. The music made him feel better.
    One day while David was playing, Saul threw
his spear at him. He tried to kill him!
    But David ran away.

Jonathan went to meet David out in a field. "My father wants to kill you," he said. "You must hide somewhere."

Then they cried and hugged each other. "We will always be friends, no matter what!" they promised.

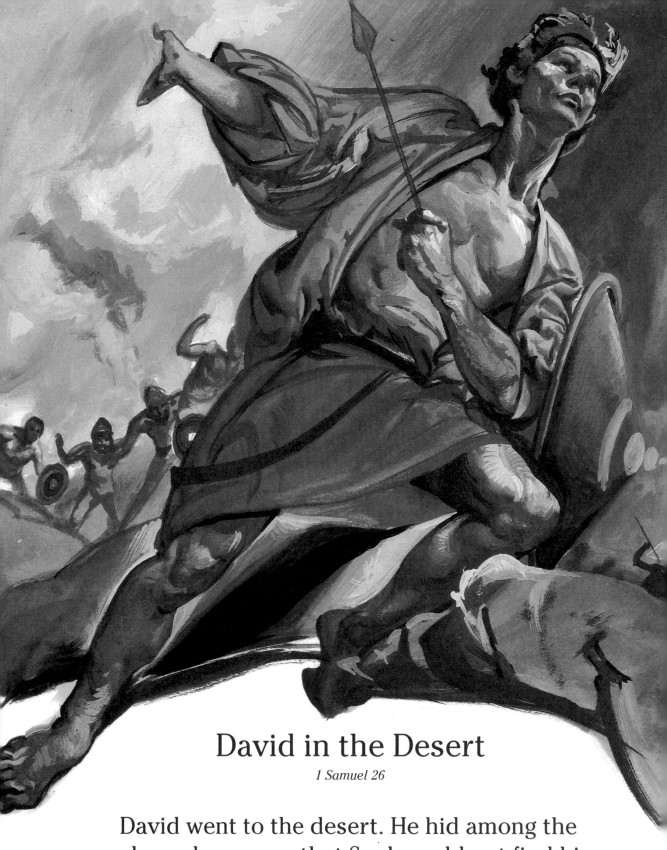

David in the Desert

1 Samuel 26

David went to the desert. He hid among the
rocks and caves so that Saul would not find him.
Six hundred men went with him, and he became
their leader.

Saul and his soldiers came after David and set
up camp in the desert.

That night David and one of his friends crept
into the camp. They saw Saul lying on the
ground asleep.

"Let me kill him!" said David's friend. "Then
you will be king!"

But David would not let him kill Saul.

David took Saul's spear and water jug and left the camp. When he was far enough away, David called out and woke up Saul.

"I could have killed you!" he said, "but I didn't. Why are you chasing me?"

Then Saul was sorry. "You are better than I am," he said.

He went home and stopped chasing David for awhile.

A Kind King

2 Samuel 5, 9

The day finally came for David to be king. All the people gathered together to watch.

The leaders poured oil on David's head, and the people shouted, "Long live the king!"

David was a kind king. "Is there anyone left in Saul's family?" he asked.

"There is only one man left," the people told David. "He is crippled in both feet, and cannot walk."

"Bring him to the palace," said David.

The crippled man was afraid when the servants brought him to David.

"Don't be afraid," said David. "I will take care of you. You will eat at my table as long as you live!"

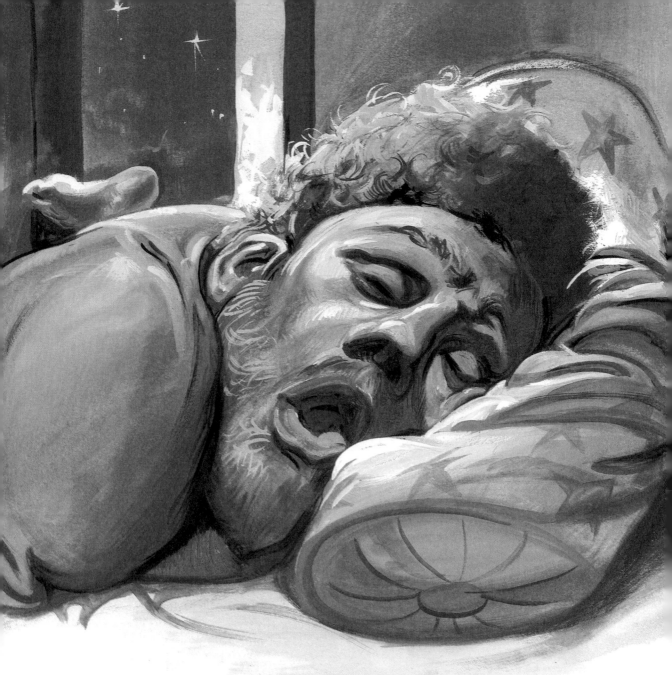

Solomon's Request

1 Kings 3–8

Solomon was David's son. One night, after he became king, God talked to Solomon in a dream. "Ask me for anything you want," God said, "and I will give it to you!"

Did Solomon ask for lots of money?

Did he ask for a long life?

No. Solomon said, "I want to be wise. Help me to be a good king."

God was pleased. "You will be the wisest man on earth," he said. "And even though you did not ask for it, I will give you riches and long life!"

Solomon built a beautiful temple so that the Israelites could come and worship God.

When it was finished, all the people came to celebrate.

Solomon prayed. "Watch over us, O Lord, and listen to us when we pray!"

Fire and Rain

1 Kings 16–18

Ahab was a wicked king. He bowed down to idols instead of worshiping God.

God sent Elijah the prophet to King Ahab, and this is what Elijah said:

"It will not rain until I say so!"

God told Elijah to go and hide by a brook.
"You can drink the water there," said God,
"and I have told the ravens to feed you."

So Elijah stayed by the brook. Every morning
and evening the ravens brought him meat and
bread, just as God had promised.

When the water in the brook dried up, God sent Elijah to Sidon, where he met a widow and her son. She had only enough food for one more meal.

"Please share your food with me," said Elijah. "God will take care of you if you do."

So the widow shared her food, and God gave them the food they needed every day.

201

The land grew drier and dustier. Food would not grow without rain.

"Where is that Elijah?" growled Ahab. He looked everywhere, but he could not find him.

Then Elijah went to see Ahab. "You have prayed to idols and disobeyed God. Now let us see who is stronger—God or idols!"

Ahab's men built an altar. They asked their idols to send fire down from heaven. They shouted and danced, but nothing happened.

"Shout louder!" said Elijah. "Maybe your idols are sleeping!"

Now it was Elijah's turn. He built an altar and then he prayed. "O Lord, let everyone know that you are God!"

Immediately God sent fire down from heaven. It burned up the altar and everything on it!

The people fell to the ground and cried, "The Lord, he is God! The Lord, he is God!"

Then Elijah prayed for rain. At first nothing happened. There was not a single cloud in the sky. But after praying seven times Elijah saw a small cloud.

"It is going to rain," he said.

Sure enough, the cloud grew bigger
and blacker. The wind began to blow.
Then down came the rain with a mighty
roar and soaked into the thirsty ground!

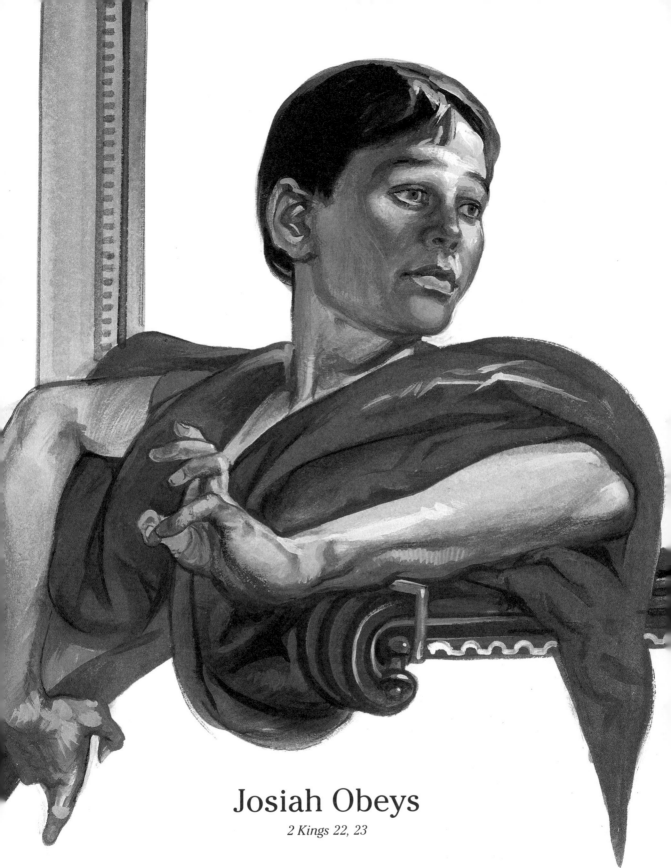

Josiah Obeys

2 Kings 22, 23

Josiah was only eight years old when he became king. He was a good king who wanted to obey God.

When Josiah grew up he noticed that the temple was shabby and broken down. He collected money to pay the workers, and soon they were busy fixing the temple.

But what was this? The workers found an old scroll in the temple. It was God's Word!

Someone brought the scroll to King Josiah. "Read it to me!" commanded the king.

As he listened to God's Word, Josiah's face grew sad. "We have not obeyed God's rules!" he said.

Josiah called all the people together, great and small. They listened as someone read the scroll out loud. "I promise to obey all of God's Word," said Josiah.

And everyone else said the same.

They Didn't Listen

Jeremiah 36–39

Jeremiah was a prophet. He had a message from God to tell the people.

His friend wrote the message on a scroll while Jeremiah talked.

But when the king read the scroll he was angry. "Why does Jeremiah say that another king will come and take us away?"

Then he threw the scroll into the fire!

No one believed Jeremiah. The king and the people kept right on disobeying God.

But Jeremiah would not stop talking.

"This man is bothering us!" complained the leaders.

"Do whatever you want," said the king.

So the leaders put Jeremiah in a well full of mud. Poor Jeremiah!

Someone finally felt sorry for Jeremiah and pulled him out.

Then the leaders put Jeremiah in prison, but he never stopped telling everyone the message from God.

One day Jeremiah's message came true. A powerful king fought against Israel and won. He put chains on the people and led them away. Then he burned their city. How they wished they had listened to Jeremiah!

The Lion's Den

Daniel 6

Daniel was an Israelite but he lived in the palace of the King of Babylon. The king could see that God was with Daniel, so he put him in charge of all the wise men of Babylon.

The other leaders were jealous of Daniel. They wanted to get rid of him. So they went to the king and told him to make this rule:

For thirty days everyone must pray only to the king. If anyone disobeys this rule, he will be thrown into the lions' den!

The jealous leaders listened at Daniel's door.

Did Daniel pray to the king? No, he did not!
Daniel prayed to God!

Right away the leaders went to the king.
"Daniel does not obey your rule!" they said.

The king was sad, but he could not break
the rule. "May your God help you!" he said.
Then they threw Daniel into the lions' den.

That night the king could not sleep. He was worried about Daniel.

Early in the morning he ran to the lions' den. "Daniel!" he called. "Did your God rescue you from the lions?"

"Yes!" answered Daniel. "My God sent his angel to shut the mouths of the lions."

The king was so happy! "Take Daniel out!" he commanded.

God did not let the lions put even a scratch on Daniel!

The Daring Queen

Book of Esther

King Xerxes needed a queen. Many beautiful women were brought to the palace. Among them was a young woman named Esther.

The king liked Esther the best. He put a crown on her head and made her his queen.

Esther had an uncle named Mordecai. He had taken care of her since she was a child.

"Do not tell anyone you are a Jew from the land of Israel," Mordecai told Esther.

And Esther obeyed her uncle.

Now there was a man in the king's court named
Haman who hated Mordecai.

"Mordecai will not bow down to me when I ride
by!" he complained.

Haman knew Mordecai was a Jew. So he asked
the king to make a new rule: All the Jews must die!

When Mordecai heard the new rule he cried and tore his clothes. Then he told Esther, "You must go to the king and try to save us!"

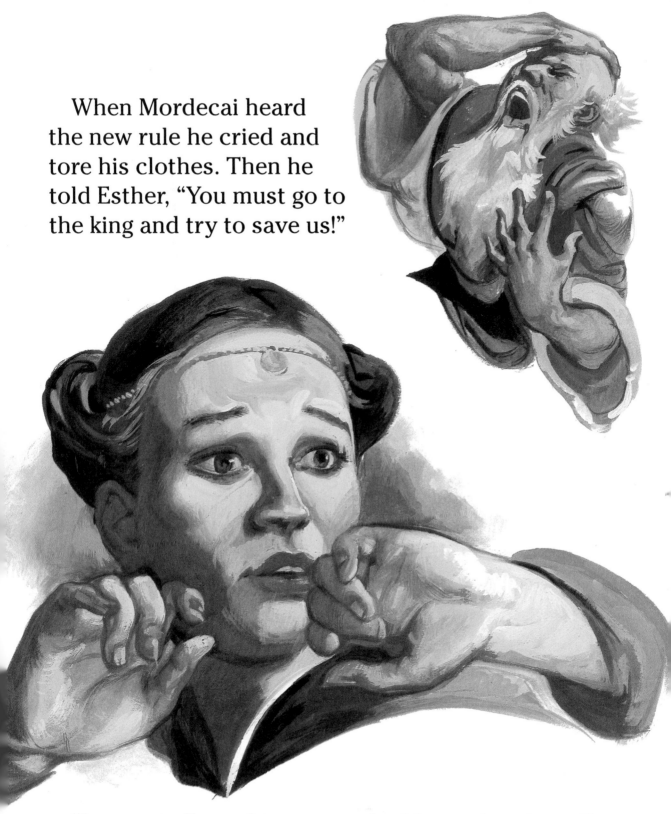

"I am not allowed to go see the king unless he calls me," replied Esther.

"You must go or all the Jews will die," said Mordecai.

"All right," said Esther. "I will go."

When Esther went to see the king he was
pleased with her. "What do you want, Esther?"
"Come to a dinner I have prepared for you," she
replied, "and bring Haman too."

While they were eating the king said, "I will give you anything you want."

"Then come to another dinner tomorrow," said Esther, "I will tell you then what it is that I want.

The next day Esther had another dinner for
the king and Haman. "Tell me what you want,
Queen Esther," said the king.

"I want my life," cried Esther, "and the life of
my people! Save us from this wicked man who
wants to kill us!" she begged.

The king was furious with Haman! He
made a new rule to save the Jews. And he
made Mordecai a leader in Haman's place.

Jonah Runs

Book of Jonah

God told Jonah to go to the wicked city of Nineveh. "Tell them I am going to punish them," he said.

But Jonah ran the other direction. He got on a boat that was going far away from Nineveh.

Then God sent a great storm. The ship was about to break into pieces.

"It's my fault," said Jonah. "God sent the storm because I disobeyed. Throw me into the water and the storm will stop."

As soon as the men threw Jonah out of the ship, the storm stopped.
Then God sent a great fish to swallow Jonah.

Jonah was inside the fish for three days and three nights. Then he prayed for help and God heard him. The fish threw Jonah up onto the dry land.

"Go to Nineveh," God said again. And this
time Jonah obeyed.

"God is going to punish you because you are
so wicked!" said Jonah to the people of Nineveh.
The people were sorry and cried out to God.
So God decided not to punish Nineveh.

But Jonah was angry.

"Why are you angry?" asked God.

"You did not do what you said you would do!" replied Jonah. Then he sat under a shelter in the hot sun and pouted.

God made a vine grow next to Jonah to shade him from the hot sun. Jonah was happy about the vine.

But then God sent a worm to eat the vine and it died. That made Jonah angry.

"You are angry because one little plant died," said God. "It is even more important that all the people in a big city like Nineveh should live and not die!"

Going Home

Book of Ezra

Cyrus the king sent a letter to all the people.
The letter said that any Jew who wanted to go
back to Israel to build the temple could go.
Many families decided to return to Israel.

When they reached the land of Israel, the
people worked hard. They built a new temple
and put a wall around the city.

Then they cried and sang for joy. "God has
brought us back to our own land," they said.